Deep
Calls
unto
Deep

Living Stream Ministry
Anaheim, CA • www.lsm.org

ISBN 978-1-57593-866-0

Living Stream Ministry
2431 W. La Palma Ave., Anaheim, CA 92801
P. O. Box 2121, Anaheim, CA 92814 USA

09 10 11 12 13 / 9 8 7 6 5 4 3

DEEP CALLS UNTO DEEP

Scripture Reading: Psa. 42:7; Mark 4:5-6;
Isa. 39:1-6; 2 Cor. 12:1-4; Acts 5:1-5

Psalm 42:7 says, "Deep calls unto deep."
Only a call from the depths can provoke a
response from the depths. Nothing shallow
can ever touch the depths, nor can anything
superficial touch the inward parts. Only
the deep will respond to the deep. Anything
that does not issue from the depths cannot
touch the depths. Others can respond deep
within to only what issues from deep within
us. When we go to a certain place and listen
to a message, the only thing that touches
us is something that has issued from the
depths of others. If nothing comes from the
depths, the help we receive is just superficial. We have to see the importance of the
depths. Anything that is not from the
depths will never reach the depths of
others. If we have never received help or
benefit in our depths, we will never have
anything issuing from our depths. If we
want to render spiritual help to others,
something must issue from our depths. If

1

we do not dig deep, we can never gain others. Unless our utterance is from the depths, we will not touch the depths in others, even though we gain their emotions and thoughts and make them cry or be happy or excited for a while. Only deep calls unto deep. Superficial expressions will not touch the depths of others.

DEEP ROOTS

One principle in preaching and receiving the word is found in the Lord's parable of the sower. While the sower sowed, some seeds fell beside the way, some on the rocky place, some into the thorns, and some into the good earth. This shows us four different ways for man to receive the word. The Lord Jesus tells us that among these different conditions, one is the rocky place. There is a little earth on the surface, but underneath there are rocks. When the seed falls into this kind of ground, it springs up quickly, but as soon as the sun comes out, it withers because of the lack of root.

What is a root? It is growth that occurs beneath the soil. What are the leaves? They are growth that occur above the soil. In other words, roots are the hidden life, whereas leaves are the manifest life. The trouble with many Christians is that, while there is much apparent life, there is very little secret life. In other words, there is the lack of a hidden life. You have been a Christian for a number of years, have you not? Then let me ask: How much of your life is hidden from view? How much is unknown to others? You stress outward works. Yes, good works are important; but apart from that manifest expression of your life, how much of your life remains hidden? If all your spiritual life is exposed, you do not have any root. Are all your virtues before God manifested before man, or is there something more that is unknown to man? If all your experiences are manifested, then all your growth is upward; there is no downward growth. If this is the case, you are a person who has only leaves without root, and you are on shallow ground.

In our Christian life it is necessary that we learn the meaning of the Body of Christ; we must learn to have a life of the Body. On the other hand, we must learn that the life given to each member of His Body by the Lord is distinctly individual. The measure that has been given to you personally by Him needs to be guarded; otherwise, it will lose its specific character and will be of no particular use to God. If that which has been specially committed to you is exposed, it will wither.

The discourse of the Lord Jesus on the Mount was most remarkable. On the one hand He said, "You are the light of the world. It is impossible for a city situated upon a mountain to be hidden" (Matt. 5:14). It is open. On the other hand He said, "When you give alms, do not let your left hand know what your right hand is doing, so that your alms may be in secret;...when you pray, enter into your private room, and shut your door and pray to your Father who is in secret" (Matt. 6:3-4, 6). On the one hand, if you are a Christian, you must come right out into the open and make a public profession; on the other hand, there are Christian virtues which you should preserve from the public gaze. The Christian who parades all his virtues before men and who does not have anything in the depth of his being has no root; he will not be able to stand in the day of trial and temptation.

We have been the Lord's children many years; may the Lord open our eyes and show us the extent to which our experiences have been hidden from public view. How much would be left if what is known by man was taken away? May God work in us so that we can take root downward.

DEEP EXPERIENCES

Writing to the Corinthians, Paul said, "To boast is necessary, though indeed not expedient" (2 Cor. 12:1). He admitted that it was "not profitable" (Gk.) for himself to write what he wrote in 2 Corinthians 12. But for the sake of others he had to do it; he was obliged to speak of "visions and revelations of the Lord." Brothers and sisters, this should be our attitude also. Many of us cannot stand the test of visions and revelations; as soon as we have a little experience, we blow the trumpet, and everyone knows about it. Paul knew that it was of no profit to himself to mention the Lord's visions and revelations. Why then did he mention them? He was forced to do so because some doubted his apostleship, and there were problems concerning the foundation of the Christian faith.

Did Paul disclose all his revelations? Far from it. He wrote, "I know a man [who is himself] in Christ, fourteen years ago

5

(whether in the body I do not know, or outside the body I do not know; God knows) such a one was caught away to the third heaven" (v. 2). He did not divulge this experience until fourteen years later. What depth there was in Paul! It would be a wonder if we could hide away something we received from God for seven years. But for fourteen years Paul never divulged his experience; for fourteen years God's church knew nothing of it; for fourteen years not one of the apostles had heard of it. Paul's roots were deep beneath the soil.

Some people would be inclined to say, "Paul, let us hear all about that experience of yours fourteen years ago. Tell us about your experience in the third heavens. It would be most helpful for us to know the whole story." But he said, "I know such a man (whether in the body or outside the body, I do not know; God knows), that he was caught away into Paradise and heard unspeakable words, which it is not allowed for a man to speak" (vv. 3-4). To this present day this experience of Paul's has not been uprooted; still no one knows about that experience.

Brothers and sisters, this matter of root is a matter of extreme importance. If you

want to have Paul's work, then you need
to have Paul's "root"; if you want to have
Paul's outward conduct, then you need to
have Paul's inner life; if you want to have
Paul's manifest power, then you need to
have Paul's secret experience. The trouble
with Christians today is that they cannot
keep any spiritual thing or any special
experience undisclosed. As soon as they
have a little experience, they have to tell
it abroad. They live their lives before men;
nothing is hidden within them. They do
not have any root. May God show us Paul's
experience, and may He lead us into
having depth!

SUPERFICIAL LIVING

In Isaiah 39 we are told that when the
news of Hezekiah's sickness and recovery
reached the Babylonian court, messengers
were dispatched with letters and a present
for Hezekiah. Hezekiah had been a recipi-
ent of the grace of God, but he was unable
to stand the test of grace. God's Word says,
"And Hezekiah was glad for them and
showed them his treasury, the silver and
the gold, and the spices and the precious
oil, and his whole armory and everything
which was found among his treasures"

(v. 2). Hezekiah could not overcome the temptation to display everything. He had just been wonderfully healed of his sickness and no doubt felt self-important and thought there were few people in the world who had had such a remarkable experience as he. After all, how many had been given such a marvelous sign at the time of their healing as the shadow on the dial of Ahaz going back ten degrees (Isa. 38:8, KJV)? In his elation Hezekiah displayed all his treasures. This means that he had not passed through the dealing of the cross. His natural life was not dealt with. It was apparent that all his roots were exposed. Whatever Hezekiah knew and whatever he had were known to the Babylonians. Because of this exposure, Isaiah said to him, "Hear the word of Jehovah of hosts: Behold, the days are coming when everything which is in your house and which your fathers have laid up as a treasure unto this day will be carried away to Babylon; nothing will be left, says Jehovah" (39:5-6). The measure in which we display things to others will be the measure of our own loss. The measure in our life that we exhibit before others will be the measure we give up in ourselves.

This is a solemn matter, and it demands our attention.

Alas, so many people cannot forbear disclosing their experiences! They have to speak to their heart's delight. This is like Hezekiah opening up his treasures to others. A brother once said, "Many of the brothers fall sick, and when they recover, they give their testimonies. I wish I could develop some sickness—but not a fatal one—and that God would heal me; then I would have something to say at the next testimony meeting." This brother's motive for healing was to be able to give a testimony. He sought an experience in order to have something to talk about. Oh! This superficial kind of living brings grave loss to us; it rules out the possibility of spiritual progress.

TESTIFYING WITHOUT EXHIBITING

Then should we not bear testimony? Yes, we should. Paul did so, and multitudes of God's children from generation to generation have done so too. But bearing testimony is one thing; delighting in exhibiting one's experience is quite another. What is our object in testifying? Is it that others may profit or that we may have the pleasure of talking? The love of hearing one's own voice and the desire to be helpful to others are two totally different things. We testify because there is a problem, and we have to speak about it. A testimony is not an after meal conversation piece. Many times while we gossip, spiritual riches leak away. When the Lord so leads, we should testify because we want to render help to others. Paul testified in 2 Corinthians 12, but he did not lightly disclose his experience fourteen years earlier. He hid his experience for fourteen years, and no one knew about it. Even when he talked about this experience, he did not disclose everything. He only mentioned the experience; he did not relate the whole story. He only mentioned the fact that he received a revelation and heard unspeakable words. He did not tell others the words that he heard. Even today, the third heaven is still a mystery, and we still do not know what it is like.

Brothers and sisters, what are our treasures? What are our gold, silver, spices, precious ointments, and precious things? What is our armory? We have to remember that gold is everything that is of God and silver is anything that is related to the redemption of the cross. Spices are the results of our wounds, precious things are the things that relate to the kingdom, and armory is the Lord's work that we have received from God and from the Lord. All these are not doctrines, biblical teachings, or theology. These are the things we have acquired through our fellowship with the Lord. When we fellowship with God, communicate with Him, and are dealt with by Him, we pick up many things. It is wrong to speak about them loosely. This does not mean that we should not testify. But we must realize that many experiences need to be hidden. Brothers and sisters, this is a crucial matter in the Christian life. Many spiritual experiences need to be hidden away and should not be exposed.

The Lord Jesus sometimes gave His testimony, but He was never talkative. It is one thing to give a testimony and another thing to be talkative. The Lord healed the sick and insisted that the story of the healing be kept secret. This charge is repeated again and again in the Gospel of Mark. Once the Lord told a certain person, "Go to your house, to your own people, and report to them what great things the Lord has done for you, and how

11

He has had mercy on you" (5:19). We may speak of the great things the Lord has done for us, but we must not publish these things abroad as items of news; this only exposes ourselves as being without any root. To be without root is to be without any treasure; it is to be without any hidden life or hidden experiences. It is essential that some of our experiences remain covered; to uncover everything is to lose everything.

Let us also remember that if we display all our treasure, captivity cannot be averted. Death and exposure go together, and spiritual dryness and exposure also go together. Even if we have to give a testimony, we must be like Paul, who boasted out of necessity "though indeed not expedient" (2 Cor. 12:1). Satan's attack often comes at the time a man is exposed. Any kind of exposure opens us up to loss. Many people are healed of their sickness, and they testify for the glory of God. But many testimonies of healing are not for the glory of God but for the glory of one's own faith. As a result, the sickness comes back. After these ones give their testimony once, they are attacked by the same thing again. This shows us that God covers those who cover their roots, and God does not protect those who disclose their roots; they will be exposed to attacks. If God wants us to testify, we still have to do it. But there are many things that ought to be hidden away. God protects what we hide before Him, and we enjoy it.

The same applies to our work. By His grace and mercy God has accomplished something through us, but remember that what He has accomplished is not a matter for advertisement or material for propaganda. If we expose the work of God, we will find that the touch of death comes upon it immediately; and the loss will correspond to the extent to which we expose ourselves. As soon as David numbered the children of Israel, death set in (2 Sam. 24). May God deliver us from this kind of exposure.

Whatever secrets we have with the Lord must be preserved. We can only move according to God's instruction within us. Only if He moves within us to reveal something, dare we reveal it. If He wants us to share some experience with a brother, we dare not withhold it, for that would be violating a law of the members of the Body of Christ. One law of the members of the

Body of Christ is fellowship. Once we suppress this law, the flow stops. We must be positive, not negative, and minister life to others. But if we are engrossed all day with ourselves and with our own things, this talkativeness and exposure opens us to assault from the enemy. I trust we shall learn what the Body of Christ is and what the flow of life among the members is; but I trust we shall also learn the need for safeguarding the hidden part we have before the Lord, the experiences which are not known to others. No root should be exposed.

As we extend ourselves deeper and take root downward, we will discover that "deep calls unto deep." When we can bring forth riches from the depths of our inner life, we will find that other lives will be deeply affected. The minute our inner being is touched, others will receive help and be enlightened. They will know that there is something beyond their knowledge. When deep touches deep, deep will respond to deep. If our life has no depth, our superficial work will only affect other lives superficially. We repeat yet again—only "deep calls unto deep."